ORANGE CO. LIBRARY
127 BELLEVIEW AVENUE
ORANGE, VA 22960
(703) 672-3811

THE STORY OF LIFE

4

Castles and Crusaders
1100 ~ 1400

MICHAEL POLLARD

Illustrated by
JOHN HUNT

AF333263

Blackie

Contents

Text © Michael Pollard 1981
Illustrations © Blackie & Son Ltd 1981

First published 1981
ISBN 0 216 90733 0
All Rights Reserved

BLACKIE & SON LTD
Bishopbriggs, Glasgow G64 2NZ
Furnival House, 14-18 High Holborn,
London WC1V 6BX

Printed in Great Britain by Cambus Litho, East Kilbride

1.
England conquered

After the Norman invasion of England in 1066, the Anglo-Saxons had a very unhappy time. William of Normandy—crowned William I of England in Westminster Abbey—shared out the Saxon leaders' land among his own followers. In exchange, they had to agree to supply him with troops when he needed them. Farmers who rented land from the new owners also had to supply soldiers. This meant that ordinary English people were little more than slaves, carrying out the orders of the hated Normans.

In the ten years after the invasion, there were *risings*[1] in almost every part of England, and each time the result was the same. The *rebels*[2] were no match for William's well-trained and well-equipped troops, and the risings collapsed. Terrible punishment followed for the rebels, their families and those who had helped them, but still the risings went on. The years of 1069 and 1070 were especially trouble-some for the Normans. Here is the story of what happened, told by someone who was there.

I don't like flat country. I never have. I was brought up in Yorkshire, where we have high moorlands and deep valleys with swift streams flowing through them. Down in the Fens you can see for miles because there are no hills at all. And the water doesn't flow; it just seeps up from the ground all around you.

My name is Edmund, and the story of how I came to the Fens goes like this. Last year I was living at home not far from York, helping my old father and mother look after their corn and sheep. They didn't have much land, but it was enough to feed us and my sister and her husband, who lived with us and helped on the farm.

We didn't travel far from home, but we had heard that there had been trouble that spring and summer in the country to the north of us. One story was that Yorkshiremen had captured the Normans' camp at York. I didn't believe it at the time, but I found out later that it was

1

true. Anyway, we were in the fields one day—it was nearly time for the harvest—when some soldiers rode up on horseback. I shouted at them because they were trampling down the corn, but they laughed and simply made their horses mill around even more. Then they rode off towards our house. My father came out to see what the fuss was about—and the next thing I knew they had gone past him and he was lying down on the path, still.

I rushed over to him, but it was too late. He was dead. The soldiers had just pushed him out of their way, and as he had fallen his head had hit a rock. And that wasn't all. Inside our barn there was a terrible noise. I climbed up to look — and inside I could see the soldiers, **dismounted**[3] now, going round breaking up all our tools and implements. Then, to make quite sure we would be ruined, they set light to the thatched roof before they rode off.

I didn't know what to do. My father was lying dead. My mother and sister were crying. My brother-in-law was still out in the fields somewhere.

Well, I found him and told him what had happened. I was so angry at what I had seen that I decided to follow the soldiers and at

least *avenge*[4] my father's death by killing one of them. The others begged me not to go, but I refused to listen. I think that I must have been sent a little mad by what I had seen. So, a day or two after we had buried my father, I set out. I just walked on and on, resting by the roadside at night, until I could find a Norman soldier to kill.

I walked for weeks, sometimes working for my food in the harvest fields and sometimes begging for bread in the villages. It was winter before I reached the flat country of the Fens, and it was there that I began to hear stories about a new English rising.

There was a man named Hereward, the stories said, who was holding out against the Normans in a monastery at Ely. He needed more men.

So I went to Ely, and a strange place it was. It was like a little hill rising out of the flat Fen land, and to get to the monastery you had to take a boat. I arrived at the *ferry*[5] at dusk. There was a boat about to leave, filled with the roughest-looking lot of people I had ever seen. They looked at me *suspiciously*[6].

"Are you a friend of Hereward's?" growled the boatman.

"Not yet," I said, "but I aim to be. The Normans killed my father and I'm looking for revenge."

"Can you fight?" the boatman growled again. "Hereward needs men who can fight."

"I come from near York," I said. "**Thereabouts**[7] we all know how to fight."

The boatman nodded and allowed me aboard. Soon, we were moored on the island, close to Hereward's camp.

At first the others didn't say much to me. Perhaps they thought I might be a Norman spy. But over the next few days, as they began to trust me, I pieced together the story of why they were all there. Hereward's idea was to hold out in his fort on the island until the Danes invaded England again. Everyone seemed sure the Danes were coming. When they did, we would break out of the island and catch the Normans between the Danish army and ourselves. It seemed a good plan to me.

All through that winter we waited. It was cold. We were half-starved. Sometimes, someone would bring us news from outside, but there was no news of the Danish invaders. Perhaps they were waiting for the new spring, we thought.

Then, one morning, we awoke to the sound of shouting. We looked out—and what we saw made our stomachs turn over. Our way across the water was blocked with ships, and, in front of us, cartloads of reed bundles were being unloaded to make a roadway across to our island so that the Normans could come and get us.

I heard later that Hereward and a few of his men escaped. I didn't. Like most of us, I surrendered and was pushed and jostled across the reed roadway, back to slavery.

2.
The building of the castles

Risings like the one led by Hereward convinced the Normans that the English were savage people who could not be trusted. The knights William of Normandy had chosen to rule over England set about building castles to protect them and their families from the **unruly**[8] natives. William himself ordered other castles to be built, such as the White Tower, part of the Tower of London, which was to protect London from invasion by river. Others were built along the south coast of England to guard the sea routes between Normandy and England.

Over eighty castles were built in the first thirty years of Norman rule, and many more were to follow. Most of the early Norman castles were built of wood but, as the knights grew richer on the rents they obtained for their land, stone was used instead. The great **programme**[9] of castle-building went on for over 200 years, some of the later ones being built on the Welsh and Scottish borders to keep out raiders from those regions. Many Norman castles are still standing today, and are among England's finest old buildings.

What was it like to work and live in a Norman castle? Edmund, whom we met in the last chapter at Ely, takes up his story.

After my adventures at Ely I was made to work harder than I had ever worked before. Norman soldiers marched a group of us to Suffolk, where we worked on the farm of a landowner called Roger Warenger. He was a Norman, and a hard **taskmaster**[10] too. I was there for about four years.

Then, one day, there was a lot of gossip on the farm. Roger Warenger owed **allegiance**[11] to the Norman Earl of Kent, Odo of Bayeux. This meant that Roger had to provide anything that Odo asked for. Odo's brother, it seemed, wanted to build a castle on his land at Berkhamsted, north of London. Odo had agreed to find the men to build it—and so he passed the message on until it reached

Roger Warenger and our farm in Suffolk. Twenty men were needed. We had no choice—we had to pack up our belongings and go.

When we got to Berkhamsted, we found that work had already started. Teams of men with shovels were making a huge mound of earth about as tall as two men. As they piled up the earth, they left a deep ditch round the outside. We set up a sort of camp outside the ditch and were given shovels and told to set to work.

I suppose there were two or three hundred of us there, but it took months to make the mound, which the Normans called a *motte*. There was a master digger who was responsible to the master builder for our work, and he was a real slave-driver. We dug in all weathers—fierce sunshine, rain, hail, even snow.

At last, the motte was finished and new groups of workmen began to arrive—sawyers and carpenters, **mortar-makers**[12] and **stone-masons**[13]. Most of the diggers were sent away, but I became friendly with one of the carpenters and he asked me to stay on as his mate. Now the really hard work was over, things were better at Berkhamsted. I watched James, the carpenter, carefully and learned how to use his tools—his axe, his different kinds of saws, and his measuring cord.

By now, a little town had grown up beside the castle site. Some of the craftsmen had brought their wives and families and built huts for them to live in. A blacksmith set up his forge to keep our tools in good shape. Some of the wives made bread and brewed ale for us, and the older children kept goats and pigs. I married a mortar-maker's daughter, Withburga, and after a while I was able to build an extra room for us on to her parent's hut, using the skills I had learned from James.

The work was not as hard as in the old days of digging. Craftsmen can't be hurried like labourers. But slowly the new castle began to rise on the motte. It had a stone **keep**[14], but the main living quarters were of timber, with a thatched roof. Round the top of the ditch we built a wall of stakes, and inside this we put up wooden buildings for kitchens, stables and store-houses. There was a new forge for the blacksmith and a barracks for soldiers. And down at the bottom of the keep there was a *dungeon* for prisoners. Even to look inside as I went past made me shiver.

I was a young man, still full of fight and hating the Normans, when I went to Berkhamsted. By the time the castle was finished I was a married man with two children. I no longer wanted to fight. I had

a new family to look after, and a new trade to follow. So when I heard that the new Lord of the castle needed carpenters to keep his new home in good shape, I decided to stay on.

The day Lord Robert of Mortain and his family moved in to the castle was a day to remember. He came with his wife, their children, ladies-in-waiting and servants, and we all turned out to watch them arrive. We had never seen such grand people before. Soldiers cleared a path for them, but we huddled in the doorways of our huts to watch them go by. They took no notice of us, of course, but we noticed everything about them, and talked about it for weeks afterwards. Playing "Lords and Ladies" became the children's favourite game for a time.

The procession went on, over the ditch—now filled with water— on a wooden bridge that James and I had helped to build, and through the gateway. As the last soldiers passed through, the bridge was drawn up. There was no more to see, and we came out of our doorways and started to gossip about the day's events. The building of the castle was finished.

3.
Inside the castle

The Norman knights did not have to work for their living. Their money came from the rents farmers paid them. They owned the land on which the towns outside the castle walls were built, and collected rents from these too, either in money or in a number of days' work each year. They were responsible for seeing that people living on their land kept the law, and fines for crime were another useful source of income.

Much of their time was spent in sport. The Normans were keen hunters, and large areas of England like the New Forest and Sherwood Forest were kept wild especially for the pleasure of the King and his friends. At home in their castles they organized *tournaments* in the sports of war—*jousting*[15] on horseback, pike-fights and contests with bow and arrow. At the back of the Normans' minds lay the thought that they might one day have to defend conquered England against an invader, and so it was sensible for their soldiers to keep in training.

Here is more of Edmund's story of life in the castle at Berkhamsted.

In the castle there was always plenty for a carpenter to do. A door would need to be re-hung, or the timbers of a roof put right. Lord Robert would walk round the castle and make a list of things that needed to be done. He would pass this on to his son, who looked after the running of the castle, and in the end a list of jobs that I could do would come down to me. Sometimes I would be sent outside the castle to repair the roof of an old couple in the village, or to help a family whose house had been damaged in a storm. The Normans didn't really like the rest of us, and they never spoke to us if they could avoid it, but they thought it was their duty to help us if we were in trouble.

The time I remember best was when the King came. It was not long before he died. I remember that, because when we heard that William was dead we all said: "But it wasn't long ago that he stayed in this very place." Anyway, he was making a journey north and stayed two nights at Berkhamsted. It made a lot of work for us, I can tell you! For days beforehand I helped to build a raised platform to go at the end of the Great Hall in the castle. Everyone in the village was brought in to help in some way—some to hang banners from the roof, others to cover the floor of the Great Hall with fresh rushes, others to clean the place up and wash the walls with lime. Lady Catherine, Lord Robert's wife, kept peeping into the Great Hall to see how we were getting on, and everyone could see she was worried in case the castle wasn't good enough for the King. Huge sides of meat and great **vats**[16] of wine were brought in. Teams of jugglers and acrobats turned up in the village, looking for somewhere to stay because they had been ordered to appear before the King. Lady Catherine watched them all perform, and sent some away because, she said, they were not good enough. She went into the kitchens and inspected all the food. Some of it was unfit for the King's table, she said, and ordered that it should be thrown away. That was good news for us; it might not be fit for the King, but it was good enough for the rest of us, we said. I don't think I have ever eaten better in my life than I did that week.

When the great day came, there was no rest for anyone. Withburga had to work in the kitchen, keeping the fire going underneath the great

pans. I was sent to check that the platform was safe, and then I had to set up the music-stands for the musicians. Even our children had jobs to do—polishing the fruit and arranging it in huge wooden bowls, or chasing the rats out of the larder. When it was time for the King and his party to arrive, we were sent out of the Great Hall to watch from the kitchen doorways. But this was not for long, because once he had come we all had to attend to the business of serving the dinner for him, Lord Robert, and the other guests.

The food they ate! It would have kept the whole village in meals for a week or more. And how they drank! It seemed strange to me that about 100 of us were bustling about, sweating and rushing and getting in each other's way, to give about a dozen people their dinner.

But afterwards—after the King, Lord Robert and his friends had gone—we went into the Great Hall to clear up. They had left enough food to keep us all alive for days. The soup that Withburga made from the bits and pieces she took away was the best I've ever tasted. After that, in our house, whenever we had a particularly good meal, we used to say: "It's like the night the King came."

4.
A hard life

For most people who lived in Britain in the Middle Ages, which is the name historians give to the centuries following the arrival of the Normans, life was very different from that of the knights and their friends. To us, even life in a castle would seem very uncomfortable and cheerless, but to the **peasants** [17] castles must have seemed like palaces. All the knights had to do, the peasants must have thought, was to collect rent, whereas only by working all the hours of the day could a peasant earn his living.

There was no education for the children of peasants. As soon as they could walk, and sometimes even before, they had to help on the land. After that, the whole of the rest of their lives would be taken up with work. It is not surprising that most peasants died young. They were simply worn out.

My name is Katherine and I was born in Wiltshire near the great Ridge Way that travellers take across the downs. The first thing I can remember is a day in the field when I was about two years old. My mother and father were sowing seeds. My father was wearing a coarse coat made of something like canvas. It was the only coat he had, so it was dirty and very worn. His shoes were worn, too—so much that his toes were sticking out of them, and every so often he would stub his toe on a stone. The seed was in a bag slung round his neck, and as he moved up and down the strip of land he took out handfuls of seed and let them fall in a shower on the ground. My mother went behind him with a wooden hoe and covered them up—but not quickly enough, because often some of the pigeons from the castle got there first. My mother's clothes were old and patched, too, and she was so tired that she could hardly walk. I didn't know then that she was pregnant again, but it can only have been a few weeks later that my sister was born.

My father reached the end of the row near where I was playing, and stopped for a rest. From his pocket he took a piece of rough brown bread, tore it in half and held out half of it to my mother as she caught up with him. They ate in silence as they looked sadly at the master's birds gobbling up the precious corn seed. Then they looked at me and started to talk. A little later, when they had finished eating, my mother came over to me and showed me how to clap two pieces of wood together to scare the pigeons away. They made me walk between them so that there was at least a chance that my mother could cover the seed before the birds swooped down.

I thought this was a good game and liked it at first. But then I got bored and wanted to go off and play by the hedge. The sun was beating down fiercely. I was hot and began to cry. But my mother and father made me carry on. "All your life will be work," my mother said. "You must learn to start now." So for the rest of that long day I walked up and down between my parents, clapping my sticks together and shouting at the birds. I have never forgotten my first day's work.

My mother was right. All my life has been work. Even now that I am a grandmother I still work as hard as ever, **salting**[18] the meat for the winter at Martinmas or tending the beehives. I think I will die soon, and I won't be sorry. They say that once you are dead you are at peace at last.

5.
The making of a monastery

Castles were not the only buildings that the Normans put up. They were very religious people, and one of their excuses for invading England was that, under the Saxons, the Church in England had become slack. After the invasion, the Normans decided that the Church must be made stronger, and so they built many great cathedrals and a huge number of parish churches over the next two or three centuries. The cathedrals and churches were run by bishops and priests brought from Normandy, and also from Normandy came monks who set up and built monasteries.

It is difficult for us to understand the Normans' **attitude**[19] to God. They were cruel and warlike people with a love of **pomp**[20] and hunting and fine clothes—things that don't seem to go with the love of God. But they really did believe that their duty to God was the most important thing in their lives. The best way to prove their love of God, they thought, was by putting up fine buildings and furnishing them with rich **tapestries**[21] and objects of gold.

One of the reasons why so many of the Normans became priests was that in those days this was the only way of learning to read and write. The only books were to be found in church and cathedral libraries, and they were often chained there to stop anyone from stealing them. Many priests, after they had learned reading and writing, left the Church and went on to other jobs.

One group of men, however, spent all their adult lives in the Church, mostly shut away from the outside world. These were the monks. After the Normans came, many monasteries were built in England. At first, most of the monks were from Normandy, but gradually they were joined by Englishmen and in 1109 an Englishman even became **abbot**[22] of the monastery at Citeaux in Normany, the chief monastery of the Cistercian Order.

By 1200, over sixty Cistercian monasteries had been built in England. This is what a monk, Stephen, had to say about life in one.

We believe that it is right to choose a life of poverty, work and prayer. Poverty does away with pride, work keeps a man healthy, and prayer reminds him at all times that his master is God.

People sometimes call us "the White Monks" because we wear a habit—a kind of cloak with a hood—made of wool that has not been dyed. In the old days, the monasteries grew rich and the monks fat, but now we have changed all that. We live as simply as we can, and as much as we can spare of what we earn is given to the poor, the old and the sick.

Our day begins when the sun rises and we go to chapel for the first service of the day, which we call *Prime*. We do not drink until this has finished and we have washed ourselves. Some days are fast days, when we do not eat at all, but usually after Prime we are allowed a drink of water. After that there are more prayers, and then the abbot may call us together to talk about the work to be done. Then we go to our places of work.

And what work! When we came to England to set up our monastery here at Fountains Abbey, in a wild part of the country which the English call Yorkshire, we had to do almost everything ourselves. We had men who were not monks—we called them "lay brothers"— to help us with the skilled jobs like masonry and carpentry, but we did all the heavy work of digging the foundations, mixing mortar, carrying heavy loads of stone and timber and building the roof. Now that the abbey itself is finished we have the task of setting out the gardens, farming the land and planting woodland.

We don't all work outside. Every morning and evening the **almoner**[23] goes to the monastery gate, where the poor of the neighbourhood gather, and sends them away with bread and ale. The infirmarian looks after the sick monks in the *infirmary*, or hospital, and often people come to him for help from the villages round about. The *librarian*[24] and his team of writers spend long hours copying out manuscripts in beautiful handwriting, decorating the pages with coloured lettering and pictures.

In the winter we have only one meal a day—some bread, with vegetables and perhaps fish or eggs. We do not eat fresh meat. In the summer, because we work harder then, we have a supper of more bread or fruit as well. There is a service of prayers before and after each meal, and in the evening we go back to work until it is time for more prayers, and then bed. We are not in bed for long, though, before the bell goes for the last prayers of the day at midnight. After that we are allowed to sleep until the sun rises again. Our beds are just mats on the floors of our rooms, with perhaps a book on which we can rest our heads.

You may think it strange that a man could give up the life of the world and choose to live in this way. But there are many good things about the life of a monk. We do not have to worry about earning money or owning land. If we are ill or unhappy, there is always someone in the monastery who will help us. We do not argue amongst ourselves, because we all agree that the main thing we must do is to obey God's laws. Life inside the monastery is very peaceful and unhurried. And, best of all, we feel close to God, and that is the best way for a man to live his life.

6.
A journey to Walsingham

England had been a Christian country for many centuries, but after the Norman conquest the English became far more **devout**[25] than before. Life was hard and often short, and they had to be prepared to die at any time. The Church taught them that if they wanted life after death they must not offend God.

They sought God's help, too, in the problems of everyday life. One way of doing this was to go on a *pilgrimage*—a journey to a holy place where prayers could be said for whatever help was needed. One of England's holy places was Walsingham, in Norfolk, where an exact copy of Mary's house in Nazareth was said to have appeared by a miracle in 1061. This is the story of a young woman, Margaret, who went on a pilgrimage to Walsingham, and what happened on the way.

From the moment he was born, my son William was a sickly child. No one knew what was wrong, but he was always so thin and pale that I cried to see him so. He could not run about like other children without stopping to catch his breath. He ate very little, and at night he would lie awake moaning as if he were in pain.

I took William to the monastery, but the monks could do nothing to help him. An old woman who lives in our village made up a **potion**[26] of herbs for him, but it did no good. My husband and I were so worried. We wanted more children, but not if they were to be sickly like William.

One day I went to the monastery again with William to see if there was anything the monks could suggest. The monk in the **infirmarium**[27] looked at William again and shook his head sadly. "It is not in our hands," he said. "Only God can save your son."

"How could He do that?" I asked.

"You must ask His mother Mary to help you," said the monk. "There is a place called Walsingham, a hundred miles from here, where you may pray to her. Pilgrims travel there from all over England."

I had never travelled more than a few miles from my home, and did not like the thought of a journey of a hundred miles. I did not know how much the journey would cost, or whether my husband would let me go. But I wanted so much to have my first son well that I told the monk that I would talk to my husband and then come to see him again.

Roger, my husband, is not a rich man but he is a miller and makes a comfortable living. He would find someone to run the mill for a few weeks, he said, and come to Walsingham with me. He would not hear of my going on my own. His mother would look after William while we were away. Roger told me to go back to the monk and ask him the way.

"You must not go alone, my child," the monk said.

"My husband will be with me," I answered.

"The roads are dangerous for two people," the monk said. "They are not so dangerous for ten or twenty. I will find out if there are any travellers to Walsingham whom you may join."

And so it was that a few months later, when work was quiet at Roger's mill, we set out one morning on horseback to ride to Peterborough. At Peterborough, the monk had told us, we would meet a party of other pilgrims at the inn, and we could travel with them across the Fens and over High Norfolk to Walsingham.

I was excited as we set out, not only because I had never travelled so far before but also because I knew that I was doing the most important thing I had ever done in my whole life. Roger did not talk much. I think he was worried in case our journey proved to be wasted. William had looked more tired and ill than ever as we said goodbye to him.

We travelled to Peterborough with some farmers who were going to market, and at the inn we met the other pilgrims. Some were like us, going to ask for help for someone else in the family. Others were going to ask for cures for themselves. Some had horrible diseases—blotchy faces or twisted legs. One kept shouting and had to be quietened by his friends.

Next day, we set off for Walsingham. It was a slow journey, because some of the travellers were on foot. In places the road was inches deep in mud—slimy mud that oozed over and into our boots.

In other places there were deep ruts that made the horses stumble and hurt the older people on foot terribly. From time to time we were joined by other pilgrims.

As we went along, we heard stories about travellers on these roads who had been robbed and killed. There were bushes too close to the road, one old man complained. Any robber could hide in them and jump out as a traveller passed. There were no signposts to show us the way, and we had no map. When we stopped for the night at an inn or a monastery we would ask the way to the next stopping-place. Sometimes there was no one who could tell us, because most people in those days had not travelled away from their own village. Once we were very frightened. A man at an inn had told us the way, but it led us into deep marshy land. Water leaked into our boots and the people at the front began to sink deeper and deeper into the mud.

We decided to turn round and go back to where we had started. When we reached the inn we asked to see the man who had given us our directions. "You won't see him again," said the inn-keeper mysteriously. Talking about this later, we decided that the man had probably intended to lead us into the marsh and then attack and rob us while we were stuck in the mud. We were more careful after that when we asked anyone the way.

It took us two weeks to reach Walsingham. Sometimes I began to despair and wondered if we would ever get there. Roger tried to cheer me up, but I knew that in truth he was as tired and dispirited as I was. Some of the old people fell ill on the journey, and one man collapsed and could go no farther.

The way from Peterborough to Walsingham crosses the Fens and goes round a great expanse of sea-water called the Wash. Then it begins to climb across a stretch of hilly country with streams to be crossed and very few villages. I was so tired with the long journey that at times I almost fell asleep on my horse, closing my eyes and seeing, behind my eyelids, the dusty road winding on ahead of us.

I must have been dozing like this when suddenly there was a shout from the front of the group. We had just come to the top of a hill. The man at the front had stopped and was pointing down at something on the other side.

"Walsingham! Walsingham!" came the message back down the line. We were there at last.

7.
Waiting for a miracle

After Canterbury, Walsingham was the most important place of pilgrimage in England in the Middle Ages, and people came there from Europe as well. Some came simply to **worship**[28] at the copy of the Virgin Mary's house. Others, like Roger and Margaret, came to ask for Mary's help for a relative. Others came to give thanks, perhaps for the birth of a child or for their **recovery**[29] from illness.

All the year round, but especially at holy times like *Christmas* and *Easter*, the streets of Walsingham were full of pilgrims. Entertainers such as jugglers and acrobats came there, too, attracted by the crowds and the possibility of earning some money. Shopkeepers and stall traders did a roaring trade in food, clothes and boots for the pilgrims' return journey.

We do not know whether travelling to Walsingham really cured people of their illnesses, but certainly the people of the Middle Ages believed it did. You can be sure that on the journey and in the square of the little town many stories were told of people who had been cured. And here is the rest of Margaret's story.

The first thing I wanted to see at Walsingham was Our Lady's house, but I was surprised to find that it was inside a chapel. When we had rested, Roger and I went there. I didn't know if the house inside the chapel was really like the house in Nazareth, but it was exciting and strange to think that it might be. For five days we went to the chapel every day and prayed to Our Lady that William might be made strong and well. On our last day we bought a little statue of Our Lady and a bottle of water that had come all the way from the Holy Land—or so the man said who sold it to us.

It was strange. When the time came for us to leave Walsingham, I didn't want to go. Perhaps I was half-afraid to arrive home again and find that the pilgrimage hadn't worked. Perhaps I was dreading that long journey back. We had been away for three weeks and our money was running out.

Monday came, and it was a great crowd of people that set out from Walsingham. Some came with us for a few miles and then turned south. Others were from London town, and they, too, left us after a couple of days' travelling. We were all tired now and made slower progress than on the outward journey. There were some children with us, and they fussed and cried. The old people grumbled. I worried. We had come all that way for a little statue and a bottle of water. I hoped it would prove worthwhile.

We were crossing the Fens one evening, hurrying to reach the next town before the gates closed and we were shut out. The line of travellers was strung out along the road, the younger and fitter ones in front and the older ones straggling behind. Roger and I were near the back of the line, because we had stopped to take a stone out of my horse's hoof. Suddenly there was a terrible fuss behind us. An old woman was screaming, and there were the voices of two or three men shouting. We stopped and looked round—and there were two rough-looking men setting about an old couple. The old man was on the ground and was being beaten over the head with a club. His wife was handing over her pack to the second *ruffian*.

"Robbers!" shouted Roger to warn some of the other men. "Stay here!" he said to me, and rode back towards the robbers and their victims. The ruffians saw him coming, and the man with the club ran into the bushes beside the road. But the other—who had the old woman's belongings in his hand—wasn't so fast. He started to run, but Roger was quicker.

"No you don't, my friend," shouted Roger, as he rode at the robber. The man went down, with the horse standing over him. Roger jumped down, seized the man's arms and twisted them behind him. With a howl of pain, the robber dropped his loot. By this time some of the other pilgrims had come up, one of them with a piece of rope which he used to **truss**[30] the robber up. Others searched the bushes for the second man, but there was no sign of him.

I was so proud of Roger, especially when the old couple—who were shaken up but otherwise unharmed—told me what a brave fellow he was and how he had saved their lives. Roger went red, and everyone gathered round and agreed that he was a real hero. Then we hurried on to the town and handed the robber over to the keeper of the **lock-up**[31]. "We've been trying to catch this young ruffian for some time," said the keeper, smiling grimly as he turned the key in the lock. "I don't think he'll be troubling travellers any more."

Roger was the talk of the town that night. By the time we went to bed the story had spread and grown, so that it was not just two men that he had fought off but a whole band of robbers, some of them armed with bows and arrows!

The excitement took my mind off William for a while, but the next day we travelled on and the worries came back again. When we reached home and went to collect him from Roger's mother's house, I was afraid to look at him. I let Roger go first.

"Tell me," I said, "tell me, is our son any better?"

"I'm sorry," Roger said quietly. "He is as he was before."

Then I cried without stopping. I thought of all the money we had spent and all the *agony* of that long journey. Most of all, I thought that this had been William's last chance, and there could be nothing else now but to wait for our son to die.

But my story has a happy ending. Very slowly, over the next two years or so, William began to get stronger. It was so slow that we hardly noticed it at first. Then, one day, I came back from the mill, where I had been helping Roger, and couldn't find William anywhere. Something must have happened to him, I thought, and I searched everywhere. I thought: I must go and tell Roger. I went out of our garden—and then I heard someone laughing. I looked around, and then the laugh came again — from high in the tree opposite our house. It was William.

"William!" I said. "You naughty boy! What are you doing up there?"

"I climbed up," he said.

Then I knew he was going to be all right.

8.
Life in the towns

If you have read Chapters 2 and 3 you will have seen how towns began to grow up outside the gates of the Norman castles. There was work inside the castles for large numbers of servants. The castle also provided work for such tradesmen as *farriers*[32], blacksmiths, builders, clockmakers and many others. These people in turn needed food and clothes, and so shopkeepers opened up to serve them.

Places of pilgrimage, like the chapel at Walsingham, also became the centres of towns. The pilgrims needed inns, food, shoes, beer and other provisions.

Then, as people began to travel more, villages and towns sprang up at crossroads and at river crossings. There would be inns for the travellers, stables for their horses, and shops to sell food for the next stage of the journey.

For all these different reasons, the towns of Britain began to grow up during the two or three centuries after the Norman invasion. Perhaps you live in or near a town that started during that time, and can find out just when it began and what the townspeople did for a living.

At first, whatever jobs they did, the townspeople still had to pay their *dues*[33] to the lord of the manor. They had to give so many days' work a year free to their lord. They had to grind their corn in his mill and give him so much of the flour as payment. They had to pay the lord for permission to marry. There were all kinds of taxes that a greedy lord of the manor could force "his" people to pay. In many ways, the people were still the lord's slaves.

But there was a way out of slavery. As towns grew bigger, their people could pay for their freedom by handing over one large sum of money to the lord. A group of the leading citizens—usually those who could drive a hard bargain—would go to the lord to discuss the matter. There would be *haggling*[34] over the price of the town's freedom, but in the end, if the lord needed the money badly enough, he would agree

to sell. Then the town would be given a charter—a kind of letter written on **parchment**[35] and signed by the lord and the leading towns-men—which said that the town and its people were now free. If you live in an old town, you may be able to find out when it received its charter.

Apart from freedom, a town charter meant a good deal more. The shopkeepers and tradesmen could elect a mayor with a **committee**[36] to run its affairs. The mayor and his committee had to see to the upkeep of the town wall and gates, bridges and streets, raising money for the work from the people of the town. Towns could run their own markets, build their own hospitals, and dig their own wells for water instead of buying water from the lord of the manor. For the first time since the Normans came, English people could run their own lives.

I am Mark, the mayor's eldest son, and I am going to tell you what our town is like. We received our charter ten years ago, when I was a toddler, and my father has been mayor for five years.

I expect that you, with your huge towns and cities, would describe our town as a "village". When you go to one of your towns, you pass through streets of houses on the outskirts before you reach the real town where the churches and shops and market-place are. Our town isn't like that. When you approach it along the road, you are passing fields and farmland one minute and then, the next, you go through the town gate and there you are—right in the middle! Very soon you come to the most important part of the town—the market-place, with the church nearby.

Our market-place is broad and open, but most of our streets would seem very narrow to you. The streets themselves slope down towards the middle, and this gutter is usually muddy—unless it is running with water. Where the houses have more than one floor (and most of them have two or three) each floor juts out over the one below, so that in some streets it's almost like walking down a tunnel. You have to be careful how you go, too, because often a housewife or her maid will empty a bowl of water or kitchen rubbish out of an upstairs window on to your head, unless you move out of the way quickly.

My father's business is brewing beer. He says he was elected mayor because he makes the best beer in the town, but I think it was because he is known to be a very fair man. Although he is the mayor, he also has to run his own business, at least until I am old enough to take over, so he has some paid *officials* to help with his work as mayor.

His main official is the town clerk, whose office is in the market-place. The town clerk's job is to collect rates and taxes from the townspeople and to make sure that any work that needs to be done is carried out properly. Not many people in our town can read or write, so the town clerk also helps people if they need to write a letter.

Then there is the town crier, whose job is to go round the town shouting out the news. Sometimes it's news about the death of a king or a victory in the French war. Sometimes it's just news about town affairs. Yesterday he went round to warn everyone that there was a thief in the town who had stolen goods from the market-place.

If the thief is caught, he will be handed over to the beadle. Some towns have a *beadle* and a number of *constables* to help him, but our

town is small enough for just one man to do the job. He looks after the town lock-up, or jail, near the church. The beadle also has to break up fights, arrest criminals, see that buckets of water are kept handy in case of fire, and make out the watch list. Every man in our town has to spend a night in turn doing *watch duty*, going round the streets looking for signs of crime or fire, and calling out the time of night every two hours.

The thought of fire breaking out is the thing that really frightens us. Our houses and shops are built mainly of wood, and are so close together that if fire broke out it would spread in no time. My father is very strict with anyone who doesn't do his watch duty properly. Once he found a man, who should have been on duty, still asleep in his bed, and sent him to the lock-up for several days.

I'm afraid you would find our streets rather messy. There are no **sewers** [37] underground, which means that all waste matter from the houses, shops, slaughter-house, workshops, breweries and animals pours into the street. In rainy seasons the rain washes it away, but in the summer the rubbish often just stays in the street and rots. You can imagine the smell, and the huge numbers of flies that feast on it! And the rats!

My father gets very angry about this. There is a rule that everyone should keep the street clean in front of his own house or shop, but very few people bother. Once my father sent the town crier round to remind people about the rule—and the result was that everyone scraped up the muck and passed it on to his neighbour! So my father paid some workmen to clear it all away, and then the townspeople complained about having to pay out more in taxes! My father was so cross about this that he said he would have nothing more to do with keeping the streets clean, and now they're as filthy as ever again.

I know that in the twentieth century some people look back on our time and think of it as "Merrie England". I think a better name for it would be "Smelly England".

9.
England v. Scotland

Like the Romans, the Normans left Scotland alone. Perhaps they did not want to risk fighting in the north of Britain before they had tamed the English. Perhaps they found Scotland too wild as a place to live. Perhaps they disliked Scotland's cold weather.

Since about A.D. 800 Scotland had suffered raids from the Danes and Norwegians, particularly on the north and west coasts. The result was that, by the time the Normans came to England, Scotland was a very different kind of country, with its own different way of life.

Scotland had its own king, but there had been marriages between English and Scottish landowning families. Some Scots owned *estates*[38] in England and some Englishmen owned land in Scotland. As England settled down after the Norman invasion, the kings who came after William the Conqueror wanted to take over Scotland and run it as part of England.

When Scotland's king, Alexander III, died without leaving a son, Edward I of England decided to claim the throne of Scotland as his own. Years of trouble followed, with the Scots under William Wallace trying to drive the English out—and nearly succeeding—while Edward I and his son Edward II fought back hard.

At last, Edward II tired of this long fight and decided to end it once and for all. In 1314 he brought together the finest army of English soldiers that had ever been seen, and set out for Scotland. Edward marched at the head of his army. At the head of the Scots was Robert Bruce, who was already a hero of earlier battles with the English. The two armies met at Bannockburn, and one of the soldiers who was there takes up the story.

It is not a happy tale I have to tell, to be sure. In the year 1314 I was an *archer*[39]—and a good one—in Lord Lovel's private army, stationed in the midlands of England. One day, news came that we were to march north. Our officers told us nothing about where we were going, but we picked up the story from some of their servants who had overheard Lord Lovel talking at his dinner-table.

It seemed that a mighty Scottish soldier, Robert Bruce, had surrounded our English castle at Stirling in Scotland. The troops inside Stirling Castle were running short of food and water, and the governor of the castle had sent a message that unless relief came by the 23rd of June he would have to surrender. We were marching north to break through the Scottish army and reach the castle.

We all thought that it was going to be an easy victory. We scoffed at the stories of the great Robert Bruce. Our English bows and arrows, we said, would soon see off the Scotsmen and their spears. We were even looking forward to the battle. The English army was a fine sight as it marched up through the hills of the border country, with our king and his nobles leading the way. We had expected to meet the Scottish army at the border, but there was no sign of them. "They've run away!" we told each other. "They're afraid to fight!"

Well, we were wrong about that. We marched on, and on the 23rd of June—the very day the governor at Stirling had said he would surrender—we reached a place called Bannockburn, just two miles from Stirling Castle. We arrived on the right bank of this river, the Bannock Burn, and camped there.

I'll remember that place until the day I die. Over to the left, on the other side of the stream, was some flat ground with, behind it, some thick woods. Ahead of us, the stream ran out through marshland. This was dangerous ground, and we were determined to keep away.

It all started quietly. We camped on the bank of the river. There was no sign of Robert Bruce and his army, and some of us thought that the Scots had run away again. We didn't know it at the time, but they were hidden in those woods on the other bank. We archers were among the first to arrive, and behind us were several thousand men— far more than the Scots had.

Soon things started to go wrong. Two advance parties of English troops set out for Stirling, one by the road and the other across country. The first was led by Sir Humphrey Bohun, a brave soldier but, as it turned out, a foolhardy one. They came across Robert Bruce inspecting his troops ready for the battle ahead. Instead of withdrawing and calling for **reinforcements**[40], Sir Humphrey ordered his advance party to charge. Of course, it was hopeless. Sir Humphrey was killed, along

30   with most of his men.

Meanwhile, the other advance party, travelling across country, had met a company of Scotsmen armed with **pikes** [41] and had been defeated.

That night, as we crossed the Bannock Burn to take up our positions for the battle, we were less cheerful than we had been before.

Next morning, both sides lined up. In front of us the Scotsmen were formed up on the slope of the hill. There were three great masses of pikemen, and behind them were more pikemen and a troop of **cavalry** [42] in reserve. In the front ranks of the Scottish army, the pikemen formed a "hedge" of spears. Our officers explained that, if we were to win, we must break down that hedge. We had three lines of cavalry in front, with the archers behind the cavalry and the **infantry** [43] behind us.

Before we knew what was happening—and before any of us had fired a single arrow—our cavalry had thrown themselves against the "hedge". Nothing happened; the Scotsmen held their ground. Our second line of cavalry went forward. Again the Scotsmen stood firm. Our third line advanced. This made no difference.

Our company of archers was ordered then to move to the side of the "hedge" and attack it from there. This meant that we had no one in front to cover our fire, and no one to protect our own side.

We were doing our best to shoot down the Scottish pikemen when suddenly, from behind us, there was a fearful noise. A troop of Scottish cavalry had attacked us, sweeping down on us from the woods. Most of my friends went down, killed or terribly injured, but I managed to escape to behind our own lines. By this time it was *chaos*[44] back there. The cavalry—those that were left—were still charging the Scottish line without any success. The archers were shooting over their heads, and their arrows as often as not fell among our own men. Our infantry had been called up from the other side of the river, so that our whole army was trapped between the Scotsmen on one side and the river on the other. We knew that the battle was lost, but we didn't know that the worst part was still to come.

32   Suddenly, there was another great noise and more Scotsmen

poured down on us from the woods. These were wild men, with the strangest collection of pikes and axes and other weapons that you ever saw. I hope I never hear again anything like the terrible cries they made as they rushed down the slope. "Slay! Slay!" they were yelling, waving their weapons and striking our English boys down in all directions.

That finished us. Our cavalry stopped charging, the archers stopped shooting, and we just ran, with the Scotsmen close on our heels. Edward and his nobles fled northwards. The rest of us were forced back to the river, where we were easy prey for the Scotsmen, or—even worse—into the marshes. Many of those who escaped the Scotsmen died from drowning. Those of us who got away had a long, weary journey home to England, travelling by night because we dared not move in daylight. But we were the lucky ones. They say that of every three men who marched north under Edward, only one came back. It was the biggest defeat I have ever seen.

10.
An old soldier's tale

After Bannockburn, the English gave up their attempt to conquer Scotland, but the English army soon had other battles to fight. In 1340, war broke out with France, and it was to last for over a hundred years.

For the noblemen who led their armies into battle, war was an adventure and an opportunity to make themselves even richer. The winning army could plunder the enemy's possessions, and the officers would take anything that took their fancy. A commander whose army won a big battle might be given a present of land by the king.

For ordinary soldiers like the archer at Bannockburn, however, there were no rewards. Even if they were not killed in battle, they were likely to die of disease. If they were wounded, there was no medical attention for them. And when they were too old or injured to fight, they were simply turned out of the army and left to look after themselves as best they could. Here is the story of one old soldier.

My real name is Thomas Tabard, but they call me Thomas One-Eye because I lost an eye in the French war. I am an old man now with not many years left, but I can remember when I was the strongest man in our village. I could fight anyone—and win. I was a blacksmith, and that's a trade to give you strong muscles.

One day when I was about twenty-five, my Lord's agent came to see me.

"I'm told you like a fight," he said.

"Yes, sir," I said, "and I always win."

"Then I have work for you," said he. "My Lord is going to fight the French, and he needs strong men with him. Are you ready to fight for England?"

"I am happy as I am," I replied.

"You're frightened to fight, then?" he snapped back. I would not be told I was frightened, so I answered: "That I am not. I will go to fight the French." I wish I had never said those words.

The year was 1346, the year of the great battle at Crécy. There was plenty of work for a blacksmith in the army, and for a time I liked the life. I was doing the same job as I had done at home, but on the battlefield, and there were new places to see and new people to meet.

I was ten years in France. It was not long before I stopped enjoying army life. I did not know whether my mother and father were still alive, and there was no way of getting news of them. The war dragged on and we went from one battlefield to the next. We ate badly. The officers kept the best food for themselves and gave us the scraps, just as if we were dogs. Sometimes there would be maggots in our meat. The bread we were given was hard and stale. The officers drank the finest wines of France, but we had only stale water to drink.

Sometimes I dreamed about running away—but where could I have gone? Even if I had somehow managed to cross the Channel and reach home, I would have had to hide from my Lord's agent. I would be a prisoner in my own home.

So I stayed in the army. I could tell you about the *victories* we had in France—but they mean nothing to me now. When we won, our officers had great feasts, but there was no feast for us. Our job was to find our dead and bury them, and try to clean up the wounded. I don't think that there is anything more terrible than a battlefield after the battle has ended: the dead lying about, the wounded groaning among them, the men without arms or legs, the men driven mad by pain.

I found out what pain was at the battle of Poitiers in 1356. For the battle, the French brought together their masses of knights in armour. Our commander, the King's son they call the Black Prince, ordered that all our men should go into battle—blacksmiths and cooks, soldiers and servants as well as the regular soldiers. Poitiers was a great English victory, but I did not know that until later.

I remember seeing the French knights advancing on us, on foot, with their bows at the ready. The next I knew, it was hours later and dusk was falling. I was lying under a hedge with one leg doubled up underneath me. I couldn't feel my foot. There was a terrible pain in my left eye, so sharp that I cried out.

There was a movement nearby, and another soldier crawled over to me. He, too, had injured his leg, and the pain as he crawled along made him draw in his breath with a hiss. He had a leather bottle of water which he handed to me.

"Take a sip of this, my friend," he said. "We are both done for. The battle is over and we are alone."

I shall never know how we **survived**[46] that night. It was bitterly cold, and because of our injuries we could not move about to keep warm. The pain in my eye went on like a fire inside my head. Then, just after dawn, we saw soldiers moving about the battlefield, looking for dead to bury. We shouted to them and they came over. We begged

for food and water, and they gave us a little of their own. One crouched down to look at me. He put his hand on my forehead and tilted my head back.

"No more soldiering for you, my lad," he said. "Your left eye is finished. I am sorry."

They took us back to camp. My friend of the night had broken his leg, but he was told that it would mend. I never saw him again. I was patched up and given a job in the officers' **quarters** [47], cleaning and doing odd jobs. But with my twisted leg and my one eye I was clumsy, and one day one of the officers shouted at me and told me to go away and never come back.

So there I was in France, with no job, no money, and the English Channel between me and home. I made my way northwards towards the coast, begging for food and shelter most of the time but sometimes doing a few days' work on a farm. But I was weak from my wounds. I couldn't work for long, and I could travel only a mile or two each day. At last I fell in with some other wounded soldiers who had been left to find their own way home. When we reached Calais we persuaded a ship's captain to take us to Dover. He had brought supplies to France for our army, and as he was going back half-empty he let us bed down in the hold.

I thought that when I reached home my troubles would be over, but I was wrong. In the ten years since I had left, there had been many changes. My father had died of a fever, and my mother was too ill to move from her bed. My dear sister had died in childbirth and her husband had moved away. I could no longer work as a blacksmith because of my missing eye, and because I could not stand for long without pain. The only work I could find was looking after the village pigs—a job that usually went to the very old or the very young, and so was badly paid. I was still a young man, but I walked with a limp and had only one eye. The only work I was fit for was old men's work.

Some of the men I had fought and beaten when I was young could now poke fun at me without fear. I once begged one of them to buy me a pot of beer. He did so—then splashed it in my face and laughed.

When my Lord came back from the war, there was a celebration at the castle, and even the village people were given a meat dinner. There were speeches about the **gallant** [48] officers and the great victory at Poitiers.

I ate my food and said nothing.

11.
A quiet life at home

While the nobles and their armies fought in France or went on the Crusades to free Jerusalem from "heathen" rule, what was life like for their wives and families at home?

The answer is that, as far as the poorer people were concerned, we do not know. The poor could not read or write, and so left behind no record of how they lived. The rich thought of the poor almost as animals, and would not have believed that anyone would ever be interested in the poor's way of life.

However, we do know something about what life was like for the people who stood between the rich nobles and the poor peasants—the **merchants** [49]. These often came from families which had risen from poverty by hard work. Although they lived more comfortably than the peasants, the way they lived tells us about the ideas of the time that affected all kinds of people—for example, the way husbands treated their wives, and parents treated their children.

This account of her life in the fourteenth century is written by the wife of a merchant living in the north of England.

I am Margaret Brown, and I have been married to my husband John for ten years. We have three children and one, Stephen, newly-born. We do not count Stephen as part of the family yet, because so many young children die. It is not good to be too fond of a baby, for you may have him only a short time.

My husband is a merchant in cloth, and spends much of his time travelling to London, York and other cities. He is a good man, and does not beat me as many other women's husbands do. He does not like me to work too hard in the house, and he gives me money to provide servants for the scrubbing and cleaning.

My mother taught me that when I married I was to obey my husband completely and to honour him above anyone else except God. I did not know John well until after we married, but I had been told

38

that he was a kind man, and this is true. But he is strict, too. When he comes home from a journey, he expects me to stop whatever I am doing and wait upon him. He does not allow our children to make a noise in his hearing, and he expects them to obey him at once without question. If they are in a room and he comes in, they must stand and be silent until he gives them leave to sit. They must not speak to him unless he has spoken to them first.

When the children are older—perhaps when they are eight or nine—they will be sent out to serve in the houses of our friends. We already have a friend's daughter living with us, helping me with the children and the cooking. It is not good for children to stay at home too long. In another house they learn better manners, are made to work hard, and become more fitted for their grown-up lives. I shall be sorry when my dear children have to leave home, just as I am sorry when my husband beats them, but I know that it is for their own good. A spoilt, wilful child will never grow up to be a good man or woman.

When my husband is away, I write to him when I know that another merchant is about to travel to the same town, and John sends me letters in the same way. I am always pleased when his letters arrive, for I have heard such terrible tales of travellers robbed on the road, or struck down with sickness in **distant**[50] places. My letters always start with "Right reverend and worshipful sir" to remind him that I have not forgotten what my mother told me. He begins his letters with the words "My own dear sovereign lady", and this tells me that he loves me above all others.

I have two servants at home, including the friend's daughter I mentioned earlier, and one in the garden, but the work of looking after the house keeps me busy all the time. One of a wife's big worries is arranging for food supplies. We live in the country, and any food we need from the city has to be ordered in good time. We buy salted herring by the barrel, six or eight barrels at a time. Fruit, too, we buy in large quantities and keep until it is needed. Other things, such as meat from our own local farmer and vegetables from the garden, we salt in our own kitchen ready for the winter. As my husband is in the cloth trade it is easy and cheap for us to buy woollen cloth, but I am always kept busy with the needle. I keep an **account**[51] of all the money I spend, and when my husband comes home he looks at it. He expects me to buy carefully, and he is angry if he thinks I have spent too much. This is right. We are not poor, but we believe that it is sinful to waste money.

When our children grow up they will marry the people we choose for them. If either of our daughters does not marry, then we will pay for her to go to a **nunnery**[52] for the rest of her life. We believe that as they are *our* children they must do what is best for *us*, just as we had to do what was best for our parents. I have no time for the French idea that people should marry "for love". It is a husband's duty to love the woman he has married, and the wife's duty to love her husband; but you cannot expect people to love each other until they have married.

"Duty" is the most important word in my life. It is my duty to look after my husband, his children and his home, and in return it is his duty to feed, clothe and care for me. It is our duty to God to keep His law and worship Him. Perhaps later **generations**[53] of people who come after us will think differently, but we believe that to do our duty is why we were born.

12.
Bartelmy Fair

Although life was hard for most people in Britain in the Middle Ages, they found ways of enjoying themselves. In the country, football was popular—but it was a very different game from the one we know today. The ball was usually a pig's **bladder**[54], and the teams would consist of all the fit men from two villages. The pitch was all the land between one village and another, and the game went on until one team was exhausted. There was no *referee*, and no limit to the amount of rough play. Broken legs and even broken heads were quite usual.

The biggest treat of the year, however, was the fair in the nearest market town, and the biggest fair in England was held just outside the city wall of London. It was called Bartholemew Fair, but "Bartholemew" was such a difficult word to say that people shortened it to "Bartelmy."

ORANGE CO. LIBRARY
BELLEVIEW AVENUE
ORANGE, VA 22960
(703) 672-0011

Bartelmy Fair began in 1133 when the king, Henry I, granted permission for it to his former court jester, Nicholas Rahere. Rahere had founded St Bartholemew's Church, and wanted to raise money for it by running the fair. Bartelmy Fair was held on St Bartholemew's Eve, August 24th, and the following day. It started as a cloth fair (and to this day there is a street named Cloth Fair close to the spot). Merchants would come from all over England to buy and sell their cloth there. But soon, other kinds of traders set up their stalls, and soon after that came the food stalls, entertainers, beggars and men looking for work. People began to go to Bartelmy Fair not only to buy goods but also for a day out. So many people went that Londoners used to say that you could meet "the world and his wife" there.

There was such excitement in our house this morning. My mother and father, sister Elizabeth and brother Richard and I were up before it was light, getting ready to go to Bartelmy Fair.

"Ann, you're the oldest, you must help the others dress," my mother said. So I found Elizabeth's and Richard's best clothes and helped them. Then I found the new dress my mother had made for me and put it on. It's not new really. My mother made it out of an old dress of hers. But it's new to me and it's my first grown-up dress.

We walked to the fair. We started soon after it was light and walked until the sun was quite high in the sky. Richard is only seven, and he began to get tired. I thought my father would get angry with him, but just in time we looked up and saw the roofs of the city of London on the skyline, and we knew we were nearly there.

By now there were hundreds of other people on the road, all going in the same direction. Some of them were carrying things to sell— baskets of fruit or rolls of cloth, bags of vegetables or bundles of clothes. Others were like us—going to Bartelmy Fair for the fun.

I have never seen so many people in my life. As we approached London there were more and more of them. The fair is held in a place called Smoothfield, where the knights practise their horsemanship and fighting skill. When we arrived, there were so many people that I couldn't see how there could be room for any more. But we squeezed in somehow.

There was so much to see that we didn't know where to start. My mother wanted to see some of the fine cloth that was for sale. My father was interested in the stalls where craftsmen were showing what they could do. Elizabeth, Richard and I wanted to go over to watch the jugglers and acrobats.

"We must all keep together," said my mother. "If we lose you, we'll never find you again."

It was Richard's fault that we got separated. There was a man playing music on a little wooden pipe, and Richard nipped in between the crowds to take a closer look. I saw him go, and followed him. But when I looked back there was no sign of my parents or Elizabeth. Richard and I were alone and lost in London town!

I said to myself, "Ann, you're the oldest. You must take care of Richard—*and you mustn't cry*." I thought that the best thing to do was to go on round the fair and enjoy ourselves, keeping an eye open for mother or father at the same time. So that was what we did. We saw a man making pots out of clay, and another making mats. We saw women spinning and weaving, and an old woman making brooms. There were dancing bears, conjurors and men walking on tight-ropes, and we saw some actors on a cart acting out a story from the Bible. But we had to hurry on when men came round for money, because we had none with us.

Still there was no sign of mother and father. We were getting tired and hungry, especially when we passed a stall selling hot sausages or black puddings. Richard began to cry. I didn't know what to do.

We had stopped beside two men who were playing a pipe and a drum. The drummer caught sight of Richard and said, "Here, what's all this fuss?"

"We're lost," I said. "My mother and father are at the fair somewhere, but we can't find them.'

"I know what to do," said the drummer. He handed Richard his drum-sticks. "What are your names?" We told him. "You bang the drum," he said to Richard, "and I'll shout out your names. Perhaps they'll hear me."

So Richard stopped sniffing and banged the drum, and the man called out "Anyone looking for Ann and Richard! Over here!" Other people in the crowd passed the message on, and it wasn't long before we saw my mother and father, with Elizabeth, making their way through. They looked worried, but when she saw us my mother smiled with relief. I didn't dare to look at my father, though. We were on our best *behaviour* for the rest of the day. But often, when we talk over old times, Richard and I remember the day he banged the drum at Bartelmy Fair.

13.
Training for a job

The master craftsmen who worked in the towns at their different trades were very proud of their workmanship. News about a good carpenter or builder or shoemaker would spread quickly, and so more work would come in. To keep out shoddy workers, the craftsmen formed guilds. Each guild was a kind of club for the craftsmen in a particular trade, and you could become a member only if you had been trained by another master craftsman. This is the story of Matthew, who trained to be a master baker.

When I was ten, my father took me to see Master Able, a master baker, to ask if I could become one of his *apprentices*[55]. When we arrived at Mr Able's shop, I had to wait outside while the two men talked about how much my father would pay Master Able to take me. At last, the door opened and I was allowed in.

Master Able was a big man with huge arms which were bare up to the elbow. There was flour on them. He put his hands on his hips and looked down at me. I was trembling, but tried not to show it.

"So you are Matthew," he said.

"Yes, Master Able," I said. My voice sounded like a whisper.

"Are you willing to work hard?"

"Yes, sir."

"You will need to rise early. A baker's work is done before it is light."

"Yes, sir."

He asked me a few more questions, and then he turned to my father and said, "He seems a lively enough lad. I'll take him. Bring him along tomorrow."

The next day my father took me back to the shop. This time I had my clothes and a spare pair of boots in a canvas bag. Master Able showed me the table in the bakery under which I was to sleep, and spoke to another boy who was mixing dough.

"This is the new young 'un," said Master Able. "His name's Matthew." Then, turning to me, he said, "He's called James, but I call him Sniffle because he's always got a cold. Ain'tcher?" he added, and to my surprise gave him a kick on the leg. Sniffle sniffed and nodded.

That was the first day of my seven years at Master Able's. The rule of the Guild of Bakers is that apprentices have to serve their masters for seven years, learning the craft. Then, if they are good enough, they are called *journeymen* and, if they can find a place that needs a bakery and if they can afford it, they can set up on their own.

For the first years of my apprenticeship, I didn't think I was ever going to learn anything. I had to do all the meanest jobs like sweeping out the shop, washing the bakery floor and delivering the bread. Once, I was helping Sniffle **knead**[56] the dough when Master Able came in and saw me. He walloped me across the hand with a wooden spoon.

"There's time enough for that later," he said. "Don't let me see you meddling again. You stick to the jobs I tell you to do."

He was a good baker and always had plenty of customers in his shop, but he was a bad master. Often he would wake us up in the morning by kicking us or jabbing a broom under the tables where we slept. I've seen him chase poor Sniffle round the bakehouse with a knife. He had agreed with our fathers to feed us, but we lived mostly on bread and pies that were too stale to sell. There was a journeyman baker called Hodd working there, too. He was too poor to start his own business, so he had to go on working for Master Able. Sometimes Master Able kicked or clouted him.

Seven years is a long time, and sometimes I was so tired after a day of humping bags of flour about or delivering bread round the town that I fell asleep over my supper. Then Master Able would jab me awake with his fork and say: "Too tired to eat? We must be feeding you too well." He was a wicked old man, but on Sundays and Holy Days, when he made us all go to church with his family, you would have thought he was the holiest man in the town.

After a while, I was allowed to knead the dough for bread or mix the pastry for the pies. Master Able usually complained about the results. "Don't rush it," he would say, aiming a cuff at my ear. "Always mix slowly." I watched him and Hodd closely when they were at work, and learned from them. Then, one day when I had been at the shop nearly seven years, Master Able said one night, "Master Hanson is coming round to look at you next Monday. He is the **president**[57] of all the bakers in the town. You'll get up early and make a loaf, a pie and some cakes. Master Hanson will look at them and taste them, and if they're good enough that will be the end of your apprenticeship. If they're not good enough, you'll be out in the street. I've no room for a bad workman."

You can imagine that I watched Hodd and Master Able even more closely for the next few days. Sniffle was coming to the end of his apprenticeship too, and we exchanged tips on how to keep our pastry light and our dough rising. That Sunday night, I hardly slept a wink. I could hear Sniffle sniffing all night, so I knew that he wasn't sleeping either. We were up even earlier than usual, stoking up the fire under the ovens and getting ready for our big day. Master Able came in.

"Now," he said, "it's all up to you. I told Hodd he can have the morning off, and I'm going to sit in this chair and watch. I want you to make our usual number of pies and loaves—without my help."

I've realized since that he would never have allowed us to do all his baking if he hadn't known we would make a good job of it. He sat there giving orders and shouting at us now and again, but didn't lift a finger to help. We kneaded and mixed, rolled and filled, sweated at

the oven and filled the tables with bread, until after about three hours we were **exhausted**[58] and the bakehouse was full of the day's baking.

Master Able picked up a pie, sniffed at it and took a bite. We watched him **anxiously**[59].

"H'm. Not too bad," he said, taking another mouthful.

Sniffle sniffed.

Then Master Hanson arrived. You would have thought the king himself had come in from the way Master Able treated him. Master Hanson was dressed in his best clothes and looked as if he were on his way to church. He took no notice of us at all. He and Master Able talked for a while about how bad trade was, and then Master Able waved his hand towards our baking.

Master Hanson also sniffed before he ate. He ate slowly, as if he were trying to make up his mind. Then, when he had finished, he

nodded, just once. Master Able had been looking worried, but now he smiled broadly.

"As I told you," he said, "they are good lads, and I have trained them myself."

Master Hanson looked at us for the first time. "You will present yourselves at the next meeting of the Guild of Bakers of this town," he said, "and be received as journeymen. A journeyman baker must be sober and quiet at all times, must attend church on Sundays and Holy Days, and must take a pride in his craft. Remember that."

I was so glad that the test was over that I felt like jumping for joy. But there was no time for that. "Now let's clean the bakehouse up," said Master Able, "or Master Hanson will think we haven't a broom in the place."

I set to work with the broom. Sniffle sniffed.

14.
Schooldays

In the years immediately after the Normans came to England, there were no schools. Very few people learned to read or write. This was not because they were not clever enough, but because they had little use for reading or writing in their lives. Gradually, however, as the great cathedrals were built, some of them opened schools, and by about 1400 it was not unusual (though it was still not common) for a boy to be sent away to school. Far more boys, however, were educated by being sent away to another family's house, like the Brown children in Chapter 11, and schools were not open to girls at all. There was just a chance that a clever boy from a poor family might be noticed by a monk and found a place at school. This is what happened to Peter, the boy in this story.

When I was ten years old I went to work in the fields belonging to the monastery near my home. My job was to weed the ground, but sometimes, if it was wet, I would be found a job inside the monastery,

mending baskets or nets or helping to move furniture. That was how I came to know Brother Paul.

Brother Paul was a kind old monk who liked to talk to people about what was happening in the world. He had lived in France when he was young and had some wonderful stories to tell about Paris, the big city there. I suppose he liked me because I was always ready to stop work for a time to listen to him.

One day, he asked me if I had decided what I was going to do with my life. I didn't understand him at first, but he went on, "You're a clever lad, too clever to spend your life in the fields. Would you like to go to school to be taught about the world?"

"But my father has no money," I said. "He could not pay for me."

"There would be no need," said the old monk. "I have a friend who has a school close by the cathedral. I will tell him that you are a clever boy and willing to learn, and he will be glad to take you in."

And so it was arranged. I went to the cathedral city about twenty miles from my home, and Brother Paul's friend took me as a pupil.

The schoolmaster, Brother Bernard, explained to me what lay ahead. I would be taught to read and write and understand **Latin**[60], which was the language in which books were written. I would also learn something about the lives of good men so that when I grew up I could copy their example. Brother Bernard would teach me about the world so that I could marvel at God's goodness in making it for us to live in. Every week, I would be tested on what I had learned, and if I failed the test Brother Bernard might have to think about sending me home.

In your schools full of books, you would have thought my school strange. There were only two books in it. In those days, before printing was invented, every book had to be written out by hand. A monk might spend his whole life copying out a few books, and so books were *expensive* and *precious*. At school, it was a great honour to be allowed to look at one of Brother Bernard's books. Usually we learned by heart. Brother Bernard would read a passage from a book, and we would repeat it after him until we knew it.

There were about twenty of us at the school, and we lived and learned in the same small schoolroom. Brother Bernard was kind to us, but the rules were very strict. If we got into trouble, he would threaten to send us home, and we knew that if that happened we would get a sound beating from our fathers. We were not allowed to play games, or sing or talk loudly. If we broke any of the rules the oldest boy would tell Brother Bernard.

We went to the cathedral for prayers every day, and to several masses on Sundays and Holy Days. I didn't really enjoy school life, but I knew that I would have to stay there. Sometimes, I wished I was back in the village with my friends and family, weeding the monastery fields instead of sitting in a stuffy schoolroom listening to Brother Bernard.

As we grew older the work grew harder. Brother Bernard told us that if we worked well we would be able to find jobs as clerks, looking after the account-books and letters of important landowners or merchants. Because of this, one of the most important subjects at the school was arithmetic. Before I went to school, I had learned to count on my fingers, but it was strange to do sums with real Roman numbers like I, II, V, X and so on. We used an *abacus*, or bead-frame, for arithmetic at first, but later on I found out how to do sums in my head.

When I had been at school for about four years, Brother Bernard took me for a walk one day round the cathedral gardens. They were beautiful gardens, full of herbs for the kitchen and plants like saffron which was used to dye cloth.

"You have been with us for four years, Peter," said Brother Bernard, "and I think we have taught you all we can. Now it is for you to decide what to do next."

He told me that the cathedral might find the money to send me to Oxford University, where I could learn more and meet other learned people. Then I would become a priest. But if I wished I could leave school now and take a job as a clerk. He knew of a landowner who needed a clerk to look after his accounts. Whatever happened, he went on, I must always remember that I was a clerk "in holy orders"— which meant that I must keep the laws of the Church. It also meant that I must not get married.

I asked Brother Bernard what it would be like at Oxford University.

"There are many men of learning there," he said, "but there are many *rogues*[61] and ruffians among the students as well. Not many years ago, there was a great battle in the streets between the students and the people of the town, and the university had to be closed down for a time."

I thought that perhaps I would be happier working as a clerk, and so Brother Bernard showed me how to write to the landowner who needed a clerk and ask for the job. Not long after that, I packed up my belongings, said goodbye to Brother Bernard and my fellow-pupils, and set out for my first job.

15.
A ruffian's story

As England grew rich, many people came from abroad to work here. Weavers came from Flanders (part of the country we now call Belgium), spice and silk traders from Italy, craftsmen of all kinds from France, and doctors came from Spain. Some of these ***immigrants***[62] did well for themselves and became rich—and this made them unpopular with the English. Merchants, who lived well, dressed in fine clothes and made no secret of their wealth, were particularly unpopular. This is what happened to one group of merchants who were unfortunate enough to meet a gang of ruffians. The leader of the gang tells the story.

When we went to Boston Fair one year, looking for some *devilment*, we had a great time. We ate and drank beer all day until we couldn't take any more, and then we set out round the town to see what was going on. We were in luck. We found this inn where there was a tremendous row going on. There was a merchant from London who said that he had been cheated by a merchant from Flanders, and they were shouting at each other so loudly that we could hear them down the street. We went in, of course, and there was the ***Flemish***[63] merchant being held back by some of the customers while the London man called him all the names he could think of. Then someone said, "There are some more Flemish men at the inn across the street. Let's go and see what they have to say for themselves!"

So we rushed out and over the road. Looking through the window, we could see this group of Flemish men sitting round a table eating their supper. Fine clothes they were wearing, too! And they were having a supper fit for a king.

These merchants make money from our English people and spend it again before our very eyes. To see them sitting there stuffing themselves with food was too much for us. We went inside, crept along the passage to their dining-room, and suddenly flung open the door and burst in on them.

You should have seen their faces! There were about ten of them against as many of us, but they were fat and sleepy and caught by surprise, so we had no trouble in getting hold of them and flinging them out into the street. By this time, a crowd had gathered, and as the merchants landed in the street they were set upon and kicked into the gutter. We threw the merchants' **bales**[64] of cloth out after them, and one or two people in the crowd who had knives slashed the bales. We kept a bale or two for ourselves, as well as a purse full of money that one of the Flemish had dropped when we burst in, and I had picked up.

After we had finished with the merchants, someone said that there were more Flemish at another inn. So we rushed off there—but the news that we were coming must have travelled faster than us, because by the time we arrived the merchants had fled.

Then we started a great hunt for them through the town, whooping and shouting as we poked into every corner and alleyway looking for them. We stopped every rich-looking man we found, to see if he was Flemish, and one of the Boston men showed me how to find out.

This is how you do it. You ask the man you've caught to say, "bread and cheese." Now, the Flemish language is different from ours, and if they try to say "bread and cheese" it sounds like "brod and case." So if any of the men we caught said "brod and case" we simply took his money and kicked him into a corner.

Then we heard that the beadle had called out the constables, so we made our way out of town as quickly as we could. It was getting dark by this time, so we stopped while there was still some light in the sky to share out what we had stolen. I was going to keep quiet about the money that I had picked up in the dining-room of the inn, but one of the others had seen me.

"Come on," he said when we had finished the share-out, "hand over the money that's in your pocket."

"What money?" I said, pretending not to understand.

In answer, he jumped on me, threw me to the ground and tore the purse away from me.

"Just for that," he said, "we'll keep your share for ourselves."

It was about ten against one, so I didn't argue. I just picked myself up, went on my way and left them to it. Still, it was a good day out.

16.
Holy war

You have read in earlier chapters about war between England and France, and between England and Scotland. But throughout the Middle Ages there was a longer and larger war—a holy war.

The trouble began at about the same time as the Norman conquest of England. An army of **Saracen**[65] horsemen rode from the east, out of the great deserts in the centre of Asia, and conquered a large part of what we now call the Middle East, including the Holy Land. In 1095, Pope Urban II made a speech in France calling for warriors to rescue the Holy Land from the Saracens, who were not Christians but Muslims.

The next year the first Crusade set out, and in 1099 Jerusalem was recaptured. But this was not the end of the war. It went on for two hundred years. The Crusaders would capture a city, and then the Saracens would win it back. Peace would be arranged, but fighting would break out again. It was not until 1291 that the Christians finally gave up.

Knights from all over Europe—including England—took part in the Crusades. When Richard I of England became King in 1189, he decided to lead an English army to join armies from France and Germany in a new Crusade. By this time, Jerusalem was again in Saracen hands, and Richard's aim was to recapture it.

Our story of this Crusade is told by Martin, who took part in it.

In the year 1189 I was living in the castle of Sir Guy Mortain as a *squire*. My father had sent me to Sir Guy when I was twelve. At first, I was a *page*, acting as a servant to the ladies of the castle and learning good manners from them. Then I became a squire, a servant to Sir Guy himself. I learned how to handle horses, how to use a **lance**[66], and how to move about wearing heavy armour.

One morning, there was great excitement in the castle courtyard. A rider had come from London with news. The new King, Richard, was calling for knights to join him in a great Crusade to free Jerusalem from Saracen rule.

"Do you think Sir Guy will go with the King?" I asked my friend, Roland.

"I hope so," he said. Like me, Roland was a squire. "It will be a chance for us to win our spurs, if he takes us with him."

Every squire hoped for the day when he would win his spurs—in other words, become a knight. One of the ways of becoming a knight was to show bravery in battle.

It was not long before we heard that Sir Guy had decided to join the King. He would take a party of knights to London to join the English army, and Roland and I were to go as well. We thought that we would be setting out at once, but we were wrong. First, Sir Guy explained, the King had to raise money for the **expedition**[67], and ships must be built for the voyage.

Sir Guy told us why we were going to the Holy Land. The Saracens had a mighty and **courageous**[68] leader whose name was Saladin. Two years before, Saladin's army had stormed into Jerusalem. We were going to win Jerusalem back.

"I should like to meet this Saladin," said Sir Guy. "They say that he is such a fine soldier that if he were not a Muslim it would be an honour to serve him."

It was in the spring of the year 1190 that we set out for London, where we were to meet Richard and his army. Along the way, people had turned out to watch us go past—and a fine sight we made on our war-horses, with our **pennants**[69] fluttering in the wind and our uniforms showing the red cross of the Crusades. Sir Guy told us what to expect.

"King Richard is a brave fighter," he said, "but he is a stern man. He will not spare anyone who does not obey orders, or who is weak in battle." We were to find out later that he was more than stern—he was cruel.

We travelled to the east by sea. We went round the coasts of France and Spain, through the Straits of Gibraltar to Marseilles in the south of France. We stopped there to take on fresh water and supplies. The journey was terrible. Few of us had ever sailed on the sea before, and when the weather was rough we were terrified—very different from the brave soldiers who had set out. We lost all track of time and place. We were exhausted by the long voyage. Only the ships' captains

knew where we were, or how much farther we would have to go before we reached the Holy Land.

From Marseilles we went to a place called Reggio in Italy, and it was here that we began to find out what a cruel man King Richard was. When we wanted supplies, he simply ordered us to rob the Italians. We paid for nothing, and anyone who asked for payment was threatened with the lance. It was the same when we moved to the island of Sicily to take up winter quarters.

In the spring of 1191, we set out again. This was the worst part of the whole journey. We met a terrible storm, and feared for our lives. King Richard was keen to reach the Holy Land and wanted to press on, but the ship's captain said that it was madness to sail on through the storm. So we landed on the island of Cyprus. Here, we fought our first battle. Cyprus was a Christian island, but Richard, who was keen for action, decided to conquer it. Then we moved on again.

At Whitsun we arrived at the city of Acre in the Holy Land. The French army, under King Philip, had already surrounded the city, and the Saracens were trapped inside. The French had been there all winter, short of food and growing weaker. If we had not arrived when we did, they could not have held out much longer.

Richard at once set about the conquest of the city. He ordered our soldiers to build wooden siege towers so that huge rocks could be catapulted over the city walls into the Saracens' stronghold. But the stories we had heard about the courage of the Saracens were true. Try as we might, we could not break into Acre. In the end, after two months, the Saracens surrendered.

I wish I did not have to tell the story of what happened next. When Acre fell, we took about 2700 Saracens prisoner. Richard agreed to let them go if Saladin paid him a large **ransom**[70], and said that the Saracens could have forty days in which to find the money. When the forty days were up, the money had not arrived, and Richard gave us the most horrifying orders I have ever heard in my life. We were to ride into the prisoners' quarters and kill every one of them.

It was our duty to obey our leader's orders, and in any case we did not dare refuse. But I had gone to the Holy Land in the hope of winning my spurs. Instead, I felt sick and ashamed at what I had to do.

17.
Disaster

The Crusades dragged on for another hundred years after the battle of Acre, and it was again at Acre that the last great battle took place. The Christians were turned out of the city. By this time the crusading armies from England, France and Germany had quarrelled among themselves and lost interest in the Holy Land.

So the Crusades had failed. They had, however, shown people in Europe that it was possible to travel to the Middle East. When the soldiers came home, merchants took their place. Ship-owners in Italy had made a great deal of money by carrying the Crusaders across the Mediterranean, and now that the Holy War was over they used their ships to carry goods instead. Such goods as silks and spices were carried to the countries of the Middle East from the continent of Asia, and it was from the ports of the eastern Mediterranean that these cargoes left for Europe.

Bales of silk were carried overland from China, across the mountains and deserts to Constantinople, where they were sold to European traders. From Constantinople the silk went by sea to Venice, and from there it was carried overland through France.

Round about the year 1333, something else made its way from China, across Asia, up to Constantinople and so on to Europe. It was not something to wear, or to eat. It was a disease—the plague.

Mark's story in Chapter 8 showed how filthy the streets of a town were in the Middle Ages. The streets of the port of Weymouth, in Dorset, were as dirty as those of any other town, and when a ship docked there one day in 1348 it was carrying black rats among its cargo, as ships usually did. The rats had in their coats fleas which were carrying the plague germs. The rats fed on the rubbish in the Weymouth streets, bred, and spread through towns and villages all over England. We know now that the disease carried by the rats was bubonic plague. The people of the fourteenth century called it the *Pestilence*. Later, it became known as the *Black Death*.

Probably nothing as terrible as the Black Death had happened in Britain before, or has happened since. Imagine if you were to open a newspaper tomorrow morning and read headlines like these:

ONE OUT OF THREE DEAD
PLAGUE WIPES OUT WHOLE VILLAGES
TOO FEW MEN LEFT TO TILL THE LAND

There were no newspapers in 1348, but if there had been, those were the headlines they might have had on the front page. And every word is true. By the time the Black Death had gone, one out of every three English people—perhaps even more—was dead, whole villages were empty and left to rot, and there were not enough people left to plough the fields.

Jane Marshall is the name of a real woman who lived through the Black Death. If she could tell us her story, this is what she might say.

At harvest-time in 1348 I was living in a village about ten miles from Bristol. My mother died when I was young, and I looked after my father and my three brothers. We had our own field, with grass for two cows, and my father and youngest brother John worked for themselves. Stephen and Nicholas, the other two, worked on the lord's farm.

I was twenty-five. My brothers Stephen and Nicholas were older than me, but John—the baby of the family—was only sixteen.

We were happy then. I kept house and helped to look after the cows and the pigs that we kept in the woods. Stephen and Nicholas brought home money from their work at the farm. John and my father grew corn and vegetables on our own plot of land. I hoped that I might marry one day, and there was a young man in the village whom I hoped would ask me to marry him.

I can't remember how it all started. But I can remember kneeling in church one Sunday and hearing Father Robert praying for the village to be saved from the Pestilence. I didn't understand what he was talking about; none of us did. But it was only a few days after that when I went to the village to shop and found the street full of little huddles of people, talking in whispers.

"What's the matter?" I asked one old lady.

"Shhh!" she said. "There's terrible news. Father Robert died in the night. They say it was by the Pestilence."

"What is the Pestilence?" I asked someone else.

"It comes like a murderer in the night," she said. "It is another name for death."

There were people who said they had heard a great wind in the night, or had smelt something on the evening air. That night, we talked about it at home.

"Father Robert was old. Old people die," said my brother Nicholas.

"It's all wild talk," said my father. "Father Robert was over seventy. It was time for him to die."

It must have been two or three days after this that I heard a noise at our door about midday. I went to see who was there, and outside I found Nicholas lying on the step, breathing hard and sweating.

There was no time—and he was too ill—to ask what was the matter. I picked up his shoulders, dragged him inside, and laid him on his straw bed. He was moaning. I cooled his brow with water, and once or twice he seemed to come round and stare at me as if he had never seen me before.

"It's Jane," I kept saying. "Nicholas, it's your sister Jane. Please speak to me."

But he said nothing. I held a cup of water to his lips, and he sipped a few drops. Then he collapsed again, staring into space and moaning.

I cannot bring myself to tell you what happened in our house between that afternoon and the moment he died a day later. Ask anyone in any family—they'll tell you. My father and other brothers came home, and we stood round Nicholas's bed looking at him. There were black marks coming out, just like bruises, underneath his skin. We all prayed, but it did no good. The next day he died.

Stephen was next. Then my father. No one who caught the Pestilence lived. The next Sunday, instead of going to church, John and I dragged the bodies of our dead family to the pit that had been dug in the village for the victims of the Pestilence. Other people were there too—husbands burying their wives, parents burying their children.

Afterwards, when we reached home, I turned to John and held both his hands.

"John," I said, "are there any black marks under my skin?"

"No," he said. "Are there are any under mine?"

I couldn't see any. We spread the house with herbs, and prayed again. I lay awake that night, wondering if I could feel the sweating begin.

18.
Into the darkness

Jane Marshall was one of the lucky ones. She did not catch the plague. Her brother John did, and she had to drag him to the village pit to join her father and older brothers. The man Jane had hoped to marry died too, with most of the other men, women and children of the village.

Jane was alone and frightened. Her story goes on:

Today, I walked round our home for the last time. I went into our garden and picked the last of the fruit. I put these and a few of my belongings into a blanket which I tied into a bundle, and then said goodbye to the place where I have lived all my life.

They say that the Pestilence rides on a horse at night, with a light so that he can choose the houses where he will stop. He has visited our house four times, and I must go away before he comes again.

I did not know where I was going. I had never been out of the village on my own, and the only road I knew was the road to market. So that was the road I took.

When I used to go to market with my father, there were always people on the road. Today, there was no one. It was strange to pass the harvest-fields still golden with corn, and no one left to cut it. The mill at the top of the hill was silent, and the miller's house was empty. At my lord's house, the gates were shut tight. I came to a little house where two children were playing in the garden. When they saw me coming, they screamed and ran indoors. As I passed, I could see them and their mother peering at me through a crack in the door.

I had a little money that my father had saved, and I thought I would go to market and buy some food for myself. But when I reached the town, its gates were closed. I knocked and shouted, and after a time a **grille**[71] in the gate was slid open and a face appeared behind it.

"What is it?" the gate-keeper said.

"I have come to market," I answered.

"There is no market. And there is no welcome for strangers in this town. Be on your way."

I understood why they had shut themselves in. Strangers like me might bring the Pestilence. But it was afternoon by now. I had eaten nothing since early morning. How was I to find food—and where was I going to rest tonight?

I knew nothing of the world beyond our market town, but there was no choice but to carry on along the road. It was rough and stony, and as I began to get tired I kept stumbling. Perhaps it would have been better, I thought, if I had died of the Pestilence with the rest of my family. This thought made me so sad that I sat down at the side of the road and sobbed. Worn out and hungry, I put my head on my blanket bundle and fell asleep.

When I awoke, I was no longer by the roadside but lying on a rough straw bed in what seemed like a stable. How had I come to be there? I sat up and looked round, and saw a man sitting at a table, reading by the light of a rush lamp. I could tell from his clothes that he was a monk.

He saw me sit up.

"Ah, you are awake, my child," he said.

"Where am I?" I said. "What has happened?"

"This is St John's Hospital," he said, "where we look after the sick and the poor. One of my brother monks found you by the roadside just before sunset, and brought you here."

Later, after he had brought me some soup and bread, I told him my story. He nodded sadly when I told him about my brothers and father. When I had finished, he said: "We have made God so angry that he has sent the Pestilence to punish us."

My father and brothers were good men, and I couldn't see how they could have made God angry, but I did not argue with the monk.

"You may stay here tonight," he went on, "but tomorrow you must go on your way. The Pestilence has been here, and only a few of my brother monks are still alive. There are so many people to be helped."

And so I come to the end of my first day away from home. Tomorrow, I must take the road again. I do not know what will become of me, but for tonight, at least, I am safe.

19.
A new world

Before the Black Death, there had been too many people trying to make a living from the land. As we have seen, many of them lived very poorly. After the Black Death had gone, there was land to spare and it was hard to find labourers to work on it. Lords of the manor could no longer treat the peasants like slaves. Instead of working for the lords for so many days a year, many peasants saved up and bought their freedom, or simply ran away to start their own farms in another part of the country. Because there was so much spare land, rents were low. Those peasants who stayed with their lords were able to demand higher wages.

The peasants who bought their freedom or ran away became farmers of a kind new in England—small farmers working, with their families, for themselves, with no lord to order them about and no need to give the lord their work. This is the story of one of them.

The Pestilence took many of the men of our village, and when it had passed on to the north country, leaving us behind, we found that there were strips of land in our open fields with no one to till them. These were shared out among the men who had survived. I now had enough land to feed myself and my family, and my good wife earned some money by keeping a few sheep. We lived more comfortably than ever before.

But it made me angry that I was still bound to work part of the time for my lord. If I had not had a wife and children, I would probably have gone away and found some fields in another village, for there was land to spare everywhere. With two or three friends, I went to the lord's agent to ask how much we must pay for our freedom.

At first, he would not hear of the idea. It was our duty, laid down by law and by God, he said, to serve the lord. We must not think that because we farmed a few strips of our own land we were free men.

This made us furious, but there was nothing that we could do about it. We went on working partly for ourselves and partly for the lord. But after a year or two, things began to change. There was talk in our village that the lord was short of money and was thinking of renting his land out to other farmers. If he did this, he would not need our work. And if he needed money, he might be ready to take some from us in return for our freedom.

We had saved a little money from the price my good wife got for her wool, and so I was able to go to the lord's agent and make an offer for my freedom. He argued about the price, but at last we agreed and I came away from his house a free man.

That was ten years ago, and since then we have prospered. We work hard, but we live well, with money to spare to buy ale and fish and have a fine dinner each day. Born a serf, I now have men working for me.

On our fields, we grow wheat one year, barley the next, and each third year we leave the soil free. The hardest work on the farm is ploughing, which takes up most of the autumn. We have two oxen to pull our plough, with one man to lead them and another to guide the plough blade.

As well as her sheep, my good wife looks after a few cows and two pigs. We keep these on the waste land that is too poor to grow crops, but when the harvest has been cut we turn the animals on to the stubble. As winter comes on, I have to decide which animals to keep for next year and which to kill for the winter's food. We can afford to feed only the best ones through the winter, for we have little hay.

The late autumn is the busiest time of the year for my wife and daughter. Enough beef has to be salted, and enough bacon **smoked**[72], to keep us through the long, dark months ahead.

When this has been done, and the great sides of meat are hanging in our kitchen, and there is wood cut and stored for the winter's fires, I can look at my family and be proud to be a free man of England.

20.
The invasion of London

Not all the peasants became free men, and not all of those who did became as prosperous as the farmer in Chapter 19. The worst-off were the "landless labourers", who rarely had a "fine dinner" or could afford to salt beef away for the winter. A law was passed to forbid the payment of higher wages to labourers, and naturally the labourers became angry. While they continued in poverty, the nobles and merchants—and even the small farmers—grew richer. The Church, too, was rich, and the anger of the labourers was turned against its bishops and archbishops.

There were, travelling about the country at this time, a number of leaders who spoke out against the richness of the rich and the poverty of the poor. One, John Ball, was a priest. Another, Wat Tyler, had been a soldier in the French wars. These men gathered round them a following not only of labourers but also of **outlaws,** [73] *poachers* [74], and criminals. The labourers wanted *justice* [75]; some of their friends were more interested in the loot that might be found by breaking into the lords' castles or bishops' palaces.

In 1381 a law was passed that, for the third time in four years, everyone in England must pay a tax of a shilling. For the poor peasants, this was the last straw, and it was the signal for the Peasants' Revolt to start. What happened next is told by an old soldier, Richard, who was there.

In the spring of 1381, I was living at the village of Eynsford in Kent. When I came back from the French War I had to take work as a labourer, with no land and poor wages. That spring, every day brought fresh news of Wat Tyler's mighty army. It was not easy to decide how much of this news was true, but it seemed that Wat and his men had seized the castle at Rochester and had then marched on to Canterbury, where they had wrecked the Archbishop's palace. Now, the rumours said, they were planning to march to London.

Perhaps we were all mad that summer. Or perhaps our lives had become so miserable that we would have done anything in the hope of making them better. Anyway, a few of us set out to join Wat Tyler and his army—though when we caught up with them on the London road I had a shock. I'm an old soldier, and know what an army on the march should look like. Wat's army looked like a gang of cut-throats, some of them dressed in uniforms they had made themselves and others just dressed in their rags. They had home-made pennants at the head of the column, and they looked to me like a mob playing at being soldiers. But we tagged along with them all the same, and after a day's march we had reached the south side of the River Thames at London Bridge.

Wat Tyler's idea was to march to the King's palace at Westminster and present him with a list of the labourers' complaints. But some of his followers had other plans. One crowd went off to Lambeth Palace, the London home of the Archbishop of Canterbury, and raided it. Another mob set free all the prisoners in Southwark and burned the prisons down. But we still had to cross the river to reach the city of London.

We could not believe our eyes when we saw the drawbridge at the end of London Bridge being lowered to let us pass through. Later, we discovered that we had friends inside the city. So we poured across, listening as we went to the news brought by the Londoners who came to meet us.

The government was frightened, the Londoners said. The young King, Richard II, had fled with his nobles and the Archbishop of Canterbury to the Tower of London, where they hoped they would be safe.

Wat Tyler and John Ball wanted to press on to the Tower to meet the King, but greed and cruelty had taken hold of their army by now. It was like a sickness. They rushed on the palace of the Savoy, near the river, cleared it of money and valuables and set it alight. Then they went on to the Fleet and Newgate prisons, freeing the prisoners and putting torches to the cells. If Wat's men came across merchants or foreigners in the streets, they robbed and murdered them. I admit that I was as bad as the rest.

The next day, we went to the Tower in the hope of meeting the King. When we stopped nearby, just outside the city wall, we heard that Richard II was coming to speak to us. Wat Tyler rode to the head

of his men. Then the city gate opened, and the young King himself rode out. He was only fourteen, and a great cheer went up from our lads—partly because it was said that the King was on our side, and partly because of his bravery in coming out to face the mob.

Wat Tyler stated his demands. He wanted all men to be made free men, all land to be let at low rents to those who wanted to farm it, and a free pardon for his rebel army.

The King agreed to all these demands. Then the mob went wild again. They broke into food shops and inns, and ate and drank all they could. Wat and some of his men went to the Tower, were smuggled in by a traitor among the guards, and beheaded the Archbishop of Canterbury and the Lord Treasurer.

In spite of this, the next day King Richard came to meet Wat again. I have often wondered if this was a trap, for within a few minutes our great victory had been turned into defeat.

Wat rode out from the front rank of his men, holding out his hand to the King. Richard was on horseback, with the mayor, Sir William Walworth, and a squire beside him.

"Be of good cheer, sire!" called Wat, shaking the King's hand.

He told the King that he had some further demands to make, and the King asked what these were. Then, suddenly, the quiet discussion became more violent. Wat raised his voice—and the next thing we saw was that Sir William, the mayor, had pulled Wat from his horse. As our leader lay on the ground, the squire came forward and finished him off with his sword.

We were stunned. Our leader was dead, and the government, which had seemed ready to give in to us, had started to fight back. We had been brave with Wat at our head. Now he was no more, the fight had gone out of us.

There had been too much bloodshed already, and I got away as quickly as I could. Many others were not so lucky, and were hunted down in the streets of London by soldiers. John Ball escaped, but I heard later that he was caught and executed.

My thoughts, as I made my way home, were bitter. We had listened to Wat and followed him—and we had failed. We were still not free. We still had no land. And now we had to face the punishments that the government and our lords would mete out to us.

The meaning of words

[1]*risings*	Violent protests of the people against their rulers.
[2]*rebels*	People who took part in risings, or rebellions.
[3]*dismounted*	Got off their horses.
[4]*avenge*	Pay back. The Normans had killed Edmund's father and he wanted to pay them back by killing a Norman.
[5]*ferry*	A boat service connecting two pieces of land.
[6]*suspiciously*	Not trusting.
[7]*thereabouts*	Round there.
[8]*unruly*	Difficult or impossible to govern.
[9]*programme*	Plan.
[10]*taskmaster*	Employer.
[11]*allegiance*	Loyalty.
[12]*mortar-makers*	People who mix up mortar, a mixture of lime, sand and water used to hold stones or bricks together.
[13]*stonemason*	A man who cuts stone to shape.
[14]*keep*	The tower which was the strongest part of a castle.
[15]*jousting*	Competitions between mounted knights.
[16]*vats*	Barrels.
[17]*peasants*	Poor people without land of their own.
[18]*salting*	Preserving meat by rubbing salt into it.
[19]*attitude*	Way of thinking about.
[20]*pomp*	Display and show.
[21]*tapestries*	Pictures or designs woven by hand in wool or silk.
[22]*abbot*	The chief monk of an abbey.
[23]*almoner*	A monk (or nun) whose job was to look after the needs of the poor and sick.
[24]*librarian*	Someone who looks after a collection of books.
[25]*devout*	God-fearing, holy.
[26]*potion*	A mixture in water.
[27]*infirmarium*	The part of a monastery or nunnery set aside for the care of the sick. Today, some hospitals are still called "infirmaries."
[28]*worship*	Prayer and praise.
[29]*recovery*	Having got better after an illness.
[30]*truss*	Tie up.
[31]*lock-up*	Cell for people who have done wrong.
[32]*farriers*	Men in charge of horses.

[33]*dues*	Taxes. Sometimes these were paid in money, and sometimes "in kind", i.e. by giving so many days' work, or so much produce from the land, to the lord of the manor.
[34]*haggling*	Arguing about a price.
[35]*parchment*	A piece of sheepskin or goatskin specially treated to make it suitable for writing.
[36]*committee*	Group of people.
[37]*sewers*	Pipes to carry away rainwater and waste.
[38]*estates*	Large areas of land.
[39]*archer*	Soldier with a bow and arrows.
[40]*reinforcements*	More troops.
[41]*pikes*	Poles with pointed heads made of iron.
[42]*cavalry*	Armed soldiers on horseback.
[43]*infantry*	Soldiers on foot.
[44]*chaos*	A hopeless muddle.
[45]*agent*	The man who looked after a lord's land and buildings. He arranged rents with the farmers and details of the labourers' work.
[46]*survived*	Came through alive.
[47]*quarters*	Parts of a camp where soldiers or their officers sleep.
[48]*gallant*	Brave.
[49]*merchants*	Traders who buy and sell goods.
[50]*distant*	Far away.
[51]*account*	List showing money spent.
[52]*nunnery*	Building like a monastery for nuns.
[53]*generations*	Children, grandchildren and so on.
[54]*bladder*	Part of the inside of an animal. A pig's bladder was blown up like a balloon and used as a ball.
[55]*apprentices*	Young men or boys being trained in a craft.
[56]*knead*	Mix with the hands.
[57]*president*	A person chosen by members of a group as their leader.
[58]*exhausted*	Tired out.
[59]*anxiously*	With worry.
[60]*Latin*	The language of Ancient Rome.
[61]*rogues*	Wicked people.
[62]*immigrants*	People who come into one country from another.
[63]*Flemish*	People from Flanders.
[64]*bales*	Bundles.
[65]*Saracen*	This was the name given at the time of the Crusades to a soldier of the Christians' enemy.

[66] *lance* — Long pole with a pointed head used as a weapon by horsemen.
[67] *expedition* — Journey.
[68] *courageous* — Brave.
[69] *pennants* — Small flags.
[70] *ransom* — Money paid for setting prisoners free.
[71] *grille* — Small opening in a door or wall with bars across it.
[72] *smoked* — Smoking meat or fish is a way of keeping it to eat later.
[73] *outlaws* — People who are on the run from the law.
[74] *poachers* — People who steal animals from a farmer's land.
[75] *justice* — Fairness.

When did it happen?

1066	The Normans invaded England.
1070	The Normans defeated Hereward at Ely.
1095	The Pope called for a holy war against the Saracens and so started the Crusades.
1096	The First Crusade set off for the Holy Land.
1098	The Cistercian Order of monks was founded in France.
1133	Bartholemew Fair was held for the first time.
1189	Richard I, "the Lionheart", became King of England and made plans to join the Crusades.
1291	The Crusades ended.
1314	The Battle of Bannockburn took place between the English and Scottish armies.
1340	Start of the Hundred Years' War between England and France.
1346	The Battle of Crécy took place between English and French soldiers.
1348	The Black Death arrived in England.
1356	England and France fought the Battle of Poitiers.
1361	The Black Death returned to England after having died out.
1381	The Peasants' Revolt.